④
10/12

④ 12/16

Apache Helicopter Pilots

By Antony Loveless

CRABTREE
Publishing Company
www.crabtreebooks.com

The World's **MOST DANGEROUS** Jobs

Editors: Mark Sachner, Adrianna Morganelli
Editorial director: Kathy Middleton
Proofreader: Redbud Editorial
Production coordinator: Margaret Salter
Prepress technician: Margaret Salter
Project director: Ruth Owen
Designer: Elaine Wilkinson
Cover design: Alix Wood

Photo credits:
Matt Carter: pages 20–21, 23
Crown Copyright: cover (top), pages 5, 7, 27
Department of Defense: pages 1, 4, 8, 9, 10–11, 13, 15, 16, 19, 24, 29
Getty Images: Choi Jae-ku: cover (bottom)
Antony Loveless: page 25

COVER STORY

◀ **COVER (top) – A British Army Apache AH-1 Longbow at its base at Camp Bastion, Afghanistan**

◀ **COVER (bottom) – Apache pilot**

PAGE 1 – A U.S. Army pilot performs final pre-flight combat checks on an AH-64 Apache Longbow helicopter in northern Iraq.

Library and Archives Canada Cataloguing in Publication

Loveless, Antony
    Apache helicopter pilots / Antony Loveless.

(The world's most dangerous jobs)
Includes index.
ISBN 978-0-7787-5098-7 (bound).--ISBN 978-0-7787-5112-0 (pbk.)

    1. Helicopter pilots--Juvenile literature. 2. Apache (Attack helicopter)--Juvenile literature. I. Title. II. Series: World's most dangerous jobs

UG1232.A88L69 2009   j623.74'63   C2009-903384-4

Library of Congress Cataloging-in-Publication Data

Loveless, Antony.
    Apache helicopter pilots / Antony Loveless.
        p. cm. -- (The world's most dangerous jobs)
    Includes index.
    ISBN 978-0-7787-5112-0 (pbk. : alk. paper) -- ISBN 978-0-7787-5098-7 (reinforced library binding : alk. paper)
    1. Apache (Attack helicopter)--Juvenile literature. 2. Helicopter pilots--United States--Juvenile literature. 3. United States. Army--Aviation--Juvenile literature. I. Title.

    UG1232.A88L68 2010
    358.4'3--dc22
                                                  2009022421

Published in Canada
Crabtree Publishing
616 Welland Ave.
St. Catharines, ON
L2M 5V6

Published in the United States
Crabtree Publishing
PMB16A
350 Fifth Ave., Suite 3308
New York, NY 10118

Published in the United Kingdom
Crabtree Publishing
Lorna House, Suite 3.03, Lorna Road
Hove, East Sussex, UK
BN3 3EL

Published in Australia
Crabtree Publishing
386 Mt. Alexander Rd.
Ascot Vale (Melbourne)
VIC 3032

CONTENTS

RIDING THE DRAGON

For most people in today's world, a day at work is not dangerous. Workers sit at desks in offices. They help customers in stores, or they make goods in factories.

For some people, however, facing danger is an everyday part of their job. The army's Apache helicopter pilots go to work each day to fight for us and to protect us. These brave men and women risk their own lives to do one of the world's most dangerous jobs.

The job of an Apache helicopter pilot is to protect ground troops —the soldiers on the ground. They do this by attacking enemy ground forces. Apache pilots are in constant danger of being shot down themselves by an enemy fighter.

Apache pilots fly the most demanding helicopter in existence. It is so complicated and difficult to operate that flying it is known as "Riding the Dragon."

One of the difficult things we have to learn is to train our eyes to work independently of each other. We wear a helmet with a monocle (an eyeglass) that displays flight and weapons information. The right eye looks at the monocle and interprets the data it provides. The left eye is free to look outside the aircraft to scan for threats.

Nick, British Army Apache Pilot

▼ The Longbow Apache helicopter uses a **radar** system (the dome on the top of the main rotor) to track targets. The Longbow radar can identify and track two priorities out of a list of 256 potential targets.

Apache pilots have a reputation within the forces as the elite of the elite—the best of the best! Only three percent of helicopter pilots qualify to fly the Apache helicopter.

THE DANGERS

The Apache helicopter is essentially a flying tank. It can inflict massive damage on an enemy and survive heavy enemy firepower. The Apache can also zero in on specific targets, day or night, even in terrible weather. It is a formidable machine for any enemy to face.

The Apache's capabilities have actually added to the danger of the Apache pilot's job. In Afghanistan, the Apache is such a terrifying machine to the **Taliban** fighters that they will do all they can to shoot an Apache down.

Because they are targeted in this way, Apache pilots keep a very low profile. For example, where quotes from Apache pilots have been used in this book, their names have been changed to protect their identities. The pilots don't want to give anything away that might be of use to an enemy.

> "I think of myself as a flying soldier, not simply as a pilot. I believe that to be effective in attack you need to feel and think like an infantry soldier—the ground soldiers who come into close contact with an enemy.
>
> The Apache's main function in battle is to attack the enemy at close range. We actually see the faces of our enemies in close-up on a five-inch (13-centimeter) square screen before we pull the trigger. It's close and it's personal, but it's them or us. That's the reality of what we do."
>
> **Mike, U.S. Army Apache Pilot**

▼ A British Army Apache flying "overwatch" from Camp Bastion, Afghanistan. The Apache is protecting the Chinook helicopters (which can be seen behind the Apache). Chinooks can carry up to 40 soldiers. With so many troops aboard, the Chinooks are a prime target for Taliban fighters shooting at them from the ground.

THE AH-64 APACHE

The AH-64 is the main attack helicopter used by the U.S. Army.

The AH-64's main fixed (permanent) weapon is a 30-mm M230 chain gun. It provides a rate of fire of 625 rounds a minute. The M230 is accurate to within 10 feet (three m) from a distance of several miles.

The AH-64 can also carry a mixture of **AGM-114 Hellfire missiles** and **Hydra 70 rocket** pods. These weapons are mounted on the helicopter's stub-wing pylons.

▶ A U.S. Army soldier loads 30-mm rounds for the M230 chain gun on an Apache helicopter.

"For nighttime operations we use the FLIR system (Forward-Looking **Infrared** system). These night vision sensors detect infrared light released by heated objects, such as a person or a hot vehicle engine. The FLIR transmits the night vision image onto our monocles.

The Apache is designed to evade **heat-seeking missiles**. It does this by reducing its infrared signature—the amount of heat energy it releases. The Black Hole infrared suppression system spreads out the heat of the engine exhaust by mixing it with air flowing around the helicopter. The cooled exhaust then passes through a special filter that absorbs more heat."

Charlotte, British Army Apache Pilot

▲ **Three Hydra 70 rockets are just visible in the rocket pod on the wing stub of this U.S. Army Apache.**

THE LONGBOW APACHE

The Longbow Apache is a modified version of the AH-64. It uses the Longbow Fire Control Radar system. Longbow Apaches flown by the British Army are currently seeing action in Afghanistan.

The Longbow Apache has a radar dome attached to the mast of the forward rotor. The radar can detect the shape of anything within the radar's range—for example, ground forces, aircraft, and buildings.

Longbow radar dome

Front rotor

M230 chain gun

AGM-114 Hellfire missile

The shapes are then compared to a database of tanks, trucks, other aircraft, and equipment to identify potential enemy targets. The targets are then shown on the pilot and gunner's monocle displays.

The Longbow Fire Control Radar is partnered with the radar-guided "fire and forget" Longbow Hellfire missile. The radar detects, identifies, and attacks with pinpoint accuracy from several miles away. The ability to attack from this distance safeguards the lives of the helicopter's crew.

The Longbow Apache uses an infrared jammer to evade heat-seeking missiles. The jammer generates infrared energy of varying frequencies to confuse the missiles and throw them off course.

Tail rotor

TRAINING

The Apache is the most technically advanced helicopter in the world. It is also the most difficult to fly.

Of the British Army Air Corps' 800 pilots, only 24 make it into the Corps' six serving Apache squadrons each year. The selection figures are similar for the U.S. Army.

It takes six months to learn to fly the Apache. Another six months are spent learning how to fight the Apache, and a final six to be passed as combat ready. That's assuming you are already a fully-qualified, combat-ready army helicopter pilot.

Raw recruits need to add even more time for basic aircraft flying training and helicopter flying training. They must also complete a course on survival, evasion, and resistance to interrogation—in case they are shot down and captured.

Before they fly a real Apache, trainees practice flying in an Apache simulator.

The U.S. Army operates a "High School to Flight School" program. This means a student can join the Army as a helicopter pilot straight from high school without a college degree. After basic training and helicopter training, a lucky few will be chosen to fly the Apache.

▲ An interior view of the cockpit of an Apache Longbow simulator.

THE CREW

The Apache helicopter's cockpit is divided into two sections. The pilot sits in the rear section, and the co-pilot, or gunner, sits in the front section. The pilot flies the helicopter, and the gunner aims and fires the weapons.

Both sections of the cockpit include flight and weapons controls in case one pilot needs to take over full operation.

One of the big difficulties that Apache helicopter pilots face is information overload! They have at least ten different new facts to register, process, and act on every few seconds. They receive information from their flight instruments. They listen to four separate radio frequencies and to the internal intercom—the system the two pilots use to talk to each other.

The pilots get information from the computers that control the weapons and from systems such as the Longbow radar.

Outside the cockpit, the pilots must look out for enemy fire on the ground, keep a visual lookout for targets, and remember the position of friendly ground forces at all times.

A sortie (or mission) can last for up to three hours—without a break!

"The Apache requires an exceptional ability to multitask. Taking an Apache into battle is like playing an Xbox, a PlayStation, and a chess grand master at the same time while riding Disney World's biggest roller coaster!"

Ed, British Army Apache Pilot

SPC CAMP
SPC SELLERS

▲ U.S. Army pilots perform pre-flight checks in an AH-64 Anache helicopter before taking off from Sather Air Base, Iraq.

▼ A U.S. Army AH-64D Apache Longbow helicopter flies a training exercise over Texas.

The main rotor, at the top of the Apache, spins four blades that are each nearly 20 feet (six m) long.

FLYING THE APACHE

The Apache helicopter has two rotors that spin several blades. A helicopter blade is like an airplane wing—as the helicopter speeds through the air, each blade generates lift.

"I maneuver the helicopter by moving the **cyclic control stick**. This causes each blade's pitch (tilt) to increase lift. Adjusting the pitch equally for all blades lifts the helicopter straight up and down. Changing the pitch for some blades creates uneven lift, causing the helicopter to tilt and fly in a particular direction.

The blades on the tail rotors have a leading edge made of titanium metal. This makes them strong enough to withstand brushes with trees. This is helpful in 'nap-of-the-earth' flying. This is when we are zipping along just above the contours of the ground. We fly this way to sneak up on targets and avoid attack.

Fortunately for us, the Apache helicopter is tough. The cockpit canopy is rigid, but the area surrounding the cockpit is designed to deform in a crash. The deformation area works like the crumple zones in a car. It absorbs a lot of the impact. If we are brought down, the Apache is capable of falling at a speed of 2,000 feet (609 m) a minute and crashing into the ground without killing the crew."

Charlotte, British Army Apache Pilot

PILOT'S EYE

One of the most difficult features to master on the Apache helicopter is the helmet mounted display (HMD). The helmet has a clip-on arm that drops the tiny screen of the monocle in front of the pilot's right eye.

Twelve different instrument readings from the cockpit are projected onto the monocle's screen. A range of other images can also be shown underneath the glow of the instruments' symbols. These images show what the Apache's cameras are seeing or provide information from a Longbow radar.

The HMD saves the pilot valuable seconds that it would take to look down at the instruments and then up again.

In each corner of the cockpit, sensors detect exactly where the gunner's right eye is looking. At the flick of a switch, the HMD locks the Apache's weapons systems to the gunner's eye-line. As the gunner's eye moves the monocle's crosshairs over a target, the weapon the gunner has selected will aim at that target. For example, if the gunner selects the Apache's 30-mm chain gun, it will swivel and aim wherever the gunner is looking.

▶ A U.S. Army Apache pilot in the cockpit. The pilot speaks to his co-pilot, other aircraft and people on the ground using the microphone on the left-hand side of the helmet.

"You suffer terrible headaches at first as your left and right eye compete for dominance, but as your eyes adjust over the months, it takes longer for the headaches to set in."

John, U.S. Army Apache Pilot

THE FORWARD AIR CONTROLLER

The Apache's capabilities are nothing without the vital help of one soldier on the ground—the Forward Air Controller, or FAC.

The FAC will be down among the infantry soldiers taking fire from the enemy. The FAC is the Apache crew's eyes and ears and will give the crew directions—what weapons are needed and where they are needed.

The FAC must know at all times where the enemy is and where friendly forces are positioned. The FAC speaks to the pilots and "talks them onto" the enemy positions. It's vital that bombs and missiles, fired from the air, are not fired on friendly forces or **civilians**.

▶ The frontline conditions in which FACs have to work. This picture shows soldiers engaging with Taliban fighters (in the trees). Shortly after this photo was taken, FAC Matt Carter called in air support from an Apache AH-64.

The FAC controls and directs all the military aircraft above the battlefield. This could include Apaches and fighter jets. The FAC must choose the right help. A 2,000-pound (900-kilogram) bomb will harm everybody nearby, not just the enemy.

> "Technically, it's defined as "Danger Close" if an FAC calls in ordnance within 100 meters (328 feet) of friendly forces. Sometimes in Afghanistan the Taliban forces are just meters from our troops and there's no choice. It's a matter of life and death for the guys on the ground, so the FAC will call in rockets as close as 50 meters (160 feet) to his own position. When it's Danger Close, the Apache gunner will ask the FAC for his initials. If anything goes wrong, it's the FAC's responsibility, not the Apache crew's."

Matt Carter, U.K. Royal Air Force (RAF) Forward Air Controller

VIEW FROM THE GROUND

Matt Carter is a Forward Air Controller (FAC) with the UK Royal Air Force (RAF). He won the **Military Cross (MC)** for his action and cool thinking while under fire in Afghanistan. Here he talks about one of the incidents that won him his bravery award:

"I knew I needed to get some air support in to deal with the Taliban fighters who were in a farmhouse and taking cover in a tree line. However, I wasn't certain exactly where all our Paras were. Also, the walls we were taking cover behind were only 30 meters (98 feet) away from the house. So, we were Danger Close and I had to be absolutely spot on with my instructions to the Apache pilots. The only way I could be sure of the situation was to run through a gap in the wall to see for myself.

The gap was about 50 meters (160 feet) wide, onto open ground. But if I didn't go, there would be no air support. The Taliban started firing at me as soon as I started running but I made it across.

I could see the house from where I was, but the Apaches were high up and further away. To them, one house looks just like another unless it's identified specifically. The choice of ordnance is vital, too. The Apache's M230 cannon is accurate to within three meters (10 feet), but we were Danger Close. I had to get our position right and then make sure the Apache was in the right position to fire."

"To identify the house to the Apache crew, I had one of the Paras fire a Light Anti-Tank Weapon (LAW) at the house. I told the crew to watch for the explosion. They did so and correctly identified the target.

When I called the Apache pilot and told him "You're clear hot," this hail of fire rained down on the house. It made the whole world around us feel like it was erupting. The power and the noise of the M230 is truly awesome. We stopped taking fire from that location immediately, and the fighters within the woods extracted out (ran away)."

A PILOT'S LIFE

When Apache pilots are on deployment in a war zone, such as Afghanistan, they will take part in different duties.

"We rotate through four specific duties. Each duty lasts for three days. First off is Very High Readiness (VHR). We have to be ready to move at a moment's notice, day or night.

The second duty involves things like test flying aircraft that have been serviced or repaired. Also we sometimes fly in replacement aircraft from Kandahar Airfield to our base at Camp Bastion. The third is "Duty Ops," which means manning the ops room and being available as backup. Here, we'll be planning missions and providing backup for the crews that are airborne."

▶ U.S. Army pilots and maintenance crew perform routine maintenance checks on a U.S. AH-64 Longbow Apache in Basra, Iraq. The helicopter will then be taken out for a test flight.

"Finally, there is Deliberate Ops, which are operations planned in advance. These might be a combat op or an escort op—when we escort Chinook helicopters, for example.

VHR is always a favorite because it has the **adrenaline** and excitement factor. You might get a call in the middle of the night and you have to be ready to move instantly. You go from being fast asleep to out flying over the troops in a matter of minutes. The whole team has to pull together. Ops scrambles the ground crew and gets them out of bed to prep the aircraft. We have to run straight to the flight line (where the Apaches sit ready for action) and get airborne as soon as possible."

Charlotte, British Army Apache Pilot

▼ **U.S. Army Apaches, part of U.S. Envoy Paul Bremer's security detail, wait for him to finish a meeting near the border between Iraq and Iran, April 2004.**

FIGHTING THE APACHE

Fighting the Apache is the job of the co-pilot, or gunner. Here, Apache pilot Nick recounts a mission over Afghanistan where he launched Hellfire missiles at Taliban forces who were hiding inside a building. On this mission, Nick was in the gunner's seat:

" The FAC told me over the radio, "Engage all remaining buildings with Hellfire; leave nothing standing." So, I confirmed his request. Hellfires need time to arm, so they are launched from some distance away. We were quite close to the target building and you don't want to be too close to the target when Hellfires detonate. So, James, the pilot, turned us around and flew us back out. Once we were about two miles (three kilometers) away, we started our run in.

I called the FAC back and told him that we were running in from the south with Hellfire so he would be prepared for when they hit.

I flicked the weapons select switch to the right for missiles. A screen on my right-hand side relayed a video feed of the target to me in real time. I lined up the crosshairs so that they were right on the middle of the building. The screen on my left told me that a missile on the right wing was ready for launch. James told me, "Clear to engage." At 1.25 miles (two km) out, I pulled the trigger. "

"There was a slight pause—no more than a second—and then the Hellfire slipped from its rail and disappeared in a rush of flame. A message appeared on my screen confirming missile launch. Now I had to keep the **laser** focused on the center of the building. It took about seven seconds for the missile to reach its target and the screen counted down in seconds to tell us how long to impact.

Dead on zero, the Hellfire struck. Right where the crosshairs were centered. Right on the center of the building."

THE BATTLE OF DONKEY ISLAND

On July 1, 2007, U.S. ground troops, supported by Apache AH-64s, were engaged with Iraqi fighters in Ramadi, near Baghdad. As the battle wore on, several of the ground troops were wounded, including Specialist Jeffrey Jamaleldine.

Jamaleldine's ground commander had called for a combat air ambulance to extract the badly wounded soldier, but it had yet to arrive. The Apache crew recalled an incident several months earlier. A British Army Apache crew had landed their helicopter in the middle of a firefight to rescue a badly wounded soldier. They did this by strapping him onto the outside wing.

Jamaleldine's life was in danger. So the Apache crew decided to act. They landed their Apache in the middle of the battle. They carefully loaded the badly wounded soldier into the copilot's seat. The copilot then strapped himself to the Apache's fuselage and crouched on the stub wing of the helicopter.

The helicopter could not be flown faster than 50 mph (80 km/h) to protect the copilot from the downthrust of the rotor blades. The Apache flew at a low level of about 200 feet (60 m) to a field hospital, where Jamaleldine was rushed into surgery.

The Apache crew didn't pause. After landing, they refueled, reloaded their weapons, and flew back to rejoin the battle. Jamaleldine made a full recovery, and the Apache's copilot was awarded the **Distinguished Flying Cross** for his actions.

▼ A U.S. Army AH-64D Apache Longbow hovers from a concealed position during a flight test near Mesa, Arizona.

◄ U.S. Armaments Repairers load a Hellfire missile onto an AH-64D Apache Longbow.

IT'S A FACT!

Apache helicopters have the ability to transmit real-time, secure (so the enemy cannot intercept it), digitized battlefield information to several places at the same time. This allows ground commanders to get an instant picture of what is happening.

Apache helicopters have a top speed of 167 mph (269 km/h).

The Apache's seats are outfitted with armor made from a strong, manmade material called Kevlar. The Kevlar armor helps absorb the impact if an Apache crashes. Weight for weight, Kevlar is five times stronger than steel.

Apache Helicopters feature a Defensive Aids Suite (DAS). This electronic device tricks enemy detection systems. It may make many separate targets appear to the enemy, or it may make the real target seem to have disappeared. DAS is used to protect the Apache from guided missiles.

Apache helicopters have a range of 300 miles (482 km) on one tank of fuel.

Apache Helicopters and the Army online
www.goarmy.com/
www.army.mod.uk/equipment/aircraft/1531.aspx

GLOSSARY

adrenaline A substance produced in the body in response to excitement. Adrenaline makes the heart beat faster.

AGM-114 Hellfire missile The Apache's fire-and-forget missile. The Hellfire requires no further guidance after launch and can hit its target without the launcher being in line of sight of the target.

civilian A person who is not in the army, air force, or navy. In a war zone, the men, women, and children who are not part of the fighting are civilians.

cyclic control stick A device that is located between the pilot's legs and controls the Apache's direction of flight.

Distinguished Flying Cross A medal awarded to any member of the United States armed forces who distinguishes themself in support of operations by "heroism or extraordinary achievement while participating in an aerial fight."

heat-seeking missile A missile that hones in on a heat source. The hottest part of any aircraft will be its engines or exhaust, so heat-seeking missiles will aim for these areas on the craft.

hydra 70 rocket An advanced, precision weapons system. Each rocket launcher carries 19 folding-fin 2.75-inch (seven-cm) aerial rockets, secured in launching tubes. The Apache gunner can fire one rocket at a time or launch the rockets in groups.

infrared A range of invisible radiation wavelengths with many uses, from home TV remote controls to night vision and thermal (heat) imaging in the military.

laser A device that generates an intense narrow beam of light. It has many uses, from DVD players and barcode scanners to target designation in the military.

Military Cross (MC) The Military Cross is an award given to British Army soldiers who have carried out an act, or acts, of extreme bravery while engaging (fighting with) an enemy on land.

ordnance Military equipment and weapons.

Paras The nickname and abbreviation of the Parachute Regiment, an elite British Army airborne assault force.

radar A way of detecting distant objects. Radar can determine an object's position and speed by sending radio waves that reflect off the object's surface.

Taliban A radical Sunni Muslim organization that governed Afghanistan from 1996 to 2001. It has been fighting a guerrilla war against the current government of Afghanistan and allied forces.

INDEX

Printed in the USA—BG